MW01103649

Madonna & Child

A Maternally Hip Baby Book

A parody
by Cathy Crimmins

ISBN 0-7871-1259-3

Printed in the United States of America

Dove Books
8955 Beverly Boulevard
Los Angeles, CA 90048

Distributed by Penguin USA

Text design and layout by Carolyn Wendt
Jacket design and digital manipulation by Rick Penn-Kraus

First Printing: October 1996

10 9 8 7 6 5 4 3 2 1

To Sean and Robin
and their adorable little brats.
Hope we run into each other
someday at Chuck E Cheese's!

Special thanks to Fernand Lamaze, Margaret Sanger, the Dionne quintuplets, *doula* Joellen Brown, child-care specialists Joanne Babaian and Sarah Babaian, Betty and Kelly Crimmins, the Goerss-Crimmins Fresh Air Fund for Only Children of Overworked Authors, Tom O'Leary, Michael Viner, Beth Lieberman, Frank Weimann, Kathy McCormack, and, of course, to my very special research associate and favorite co-author, Tom Maeder, for inestimable help and inspiration. I also owe a debt of gratitude and love to the amazingly hardheaded Alan Forman for opening up his (and my) eyes again.

Table of Contents

This book is divided into trimesters, but I promise that the first section won't make you nauseated!

Part One

The First Trimester...

Part Two
The Second Trimester...

Part Three
The Third Trimester...

Dear Expectant Fans,

Here is the event—and the book—you've been waiting for. It's bigger than any CD, music video, or movie could ever be. It's not photogenic—it's GENETIC. If you enjoyed my book, Sex, *you're going to love this fabulous sequel that deals exclusively with procreation.* Madonna and Child *will tell you everything you ever wanted to know about having a celebrity baby but were afraid to ask.*

Why would I want to bare all and tell what it's really like to give birth to the most famous infant in the world? Several reasons:

1. Money. Let's face it—the Madonnaketeer is going to need a little extra spending money at Harvard.

2. Posterity. Too many of my friends have told me that you never really write down all that stuff in your baby book. Why? Because no one is paying you for it. I'm not going to make that mistake. If I have a publisher who's given me a contract to write this thing, you can damned well be sure that I—or one of my flunkies—will finish it.

3. Kicks. Yeah, you read it right. I've hired so many nannies, I have plenty of time on my hands. I can only work on my abs for three or four hours a day, and then I want something meaningful to do in all those long postpartum hours.

4. Community need. The community of celebrities, I mean. There are a lot of books out there for ordinary folks who breed—*What to Expect When You're Expecting,* Dr. Spock, Penelope Leach. But what about the special needs of celebrity parents? Does anyone let them know the right way to breast-feed on the Concorde? Do other books tell about kid-friendly restaurants in Cannes, or explain how to get yourself a prenatal P.R. consultant?

So thanks for caring about my career and my progeny. I know you'll enjoy this book, because, after all, it's about the most famous girl (and baby) in the world.

Ciao!

Madonna

Part One

THE FIRST TRIMESTER...

...in which I fill you in on

how to pick up semen,

how to decide when you're ready to have

a kid, how to choose the perfect

baby name, what to expect when

you're expecting a star...

and I also reveal my all-time

Mommy Dearest role models

and favorite *cinema maternité.*

Sooner or later, your DNA is gonna be mine, or...

How to Pick up Semen

Spermatozoa—it's such weird stuff. Messy. A little smelly. It frequently ruins silk underwear. But if a girl wants to get knocked up, she must seek an out-of-condom experience. I had hoped to hold out long enough to avoid the hassle and get myself cloned. At 37, I finally realized technology wasn't catching up fast enough—it was time to go hunting for the right genetic material and do it the old-fashioned way.

Before I could embark on that joyous first step toward motherhood, I had to decide what kind of man should be father of my child. An awesome role, really.

Some candidates for Sperm Donor:

The First Husband

A traditional choice, but not good enough for me.

Some men were born to be ex-husbands, like my first spouse. Sexy, volatile, cute—but the father of my baby? No way. Anyway, it's just too geeky to go right out and reproduce with the first guy you marry. Like *Dead Dad Walking,* okay? I'm glad I waited—otherwise I would have denied myself the pleasure of watching some other woman get miserable raising his brats.

FOR YOU-KNOW-WHO: A LITTLE KIDDIE RHYME

Warren, Warren, *Shampoo* guy,
Shtupped the girls and made them cry.
When the girls came back to stay,
Warren Darling ran away.

The Famous Older Actor

I love a man when his neck starts to wobble, don't you? Guys are just adorable during a midlife crisis—they let you put them in documentaries and generally will make a fool out of themselves in all sorts of ways for love. But I couldn't have a baby with Dick Tracy, not in a million years! First, there's that problem of old sperm. Then, I just knew he would get heavily into the fatherhood trip, and before long I'd be playing second fiddle to the adorable progeny. Look at his poor young wife. One minute she was a sexy young thing humping John Cusack—now she's a matron playing nice girls opposite hubby and that other wobble-neck, Michael Douglas.

Girlfriends

Every woman has fantasies about starting a family with some really good girlfriends, and I'm no exception. But the mechanics are too complicated. Even a strap-on won't get the job done, and none of my friends cook well enough to know how to baste a turkey.

NBA Star

Buns of steel, brains of a bird. For a while there I thought I wanted my children to be athletic, but I also want them to finish high school. Plus I hate a guy who looks better than I do in lingerie, and the fumes from his hair dye were a real turn-off, too. In a way I'm sorry it didn't work out, because I like a guy who can dribble *and* shoot real straight.

Priest

Tempting. I do like a virgin, and I do want to raise my child to be a good Catholic. But most priests are gay, anyway, right?

Sperm Bank

I've had sex with so many good-looking, virile young guys—exactly the types who donate to those places. You know—did him, done him, had him. It all gets so boooooring! That's why I just didn't feel right buying

Confidential to Dennis Rodman

TOP TEN REASONS I'M GLAD I DIDN'T HAVE YOUR BABY

1. Your butt isn't as tight as you think it is.
2. You would show up naked at Little League games and embarrass our kid.
3. I'd be forever trying to get lipstick stains off our kid's onesies.
4. I believe children should know the natural hair color of at least one of their parents.
5. You'd always be complaining that our baby put runs in your pantyhose.
6. I hate putting babies in snowsuits, and Chicago is a snowy town.
7. I would never have a baby with a guy who told the world I'm only average in bed.
8. You would always be borrowing my nursing bras.
9. I prefer paying the salary of my kid's father, and you earn too much.
10. You would probably make me call it Dennis, Jr.

off-the-rack semen. A girl doesn't want to see herself coming and going—I want designer genes.

Personal Entourage-type Guys

Bingo! Get yourself a good post-bonk, prenatal contract with exclusive custody of the kid, and just have fun! I recommend conceiving with a personal slave, er...servant. You will always have more power and more money than Daddy, and isn't that what all women want, anyway? Believe me, procreational personal training is the most fun I've ever had! I particularly recommend the pelvic thrusts.

What If... A Formula for Choosing My Sperm Donor

It's a drag to be famous and rich—I could have had almost anybody, and don't think I didn't consider all of them. Below, a very partial list of other possibilities:

Me + Pee-wee Herman

Pluses: Children's programming opportunities, very few further sexual demands on me
Minuses: Child's vocal cords and wardrobe choices might be strange

Me + Arnold Schwarzenegger

Pluses: Kid would have great abs, possible action/sitcom deal with three of us, boffo box office appeal
Minuses: Maria Shriver (still has access to guys who can put you in cement shoes)

Me + Brad Pitt

Pluses: Kid would have great hair, cute buns, definitely Oscar genetic material
Minuses: Don't need a dad who makes as much money as I do—could get messy

Me + Bill Gates

Pluses: Totally wired nursery, good IQ genes
Minuses: If I have to tell you, you're too nerdy to understand

Me + George Clooney

Pluses: In an emergency, I'd take Batman any day
Minuses: His aunt Rosemary got real blimpy when she got old—do I want that for my kid?

Me + Bill Clinton

Pluses: High energy level, likes to feel my pain
Minuses: Too old; french-fried butt

Me + Ross Perot

Pluses: Worth billions, a certain openness
Minuses: Big ears, whiney voice, mental illness, advanced age

Me + David Letterman

Pluses: Possibility of on-air birth exposure
Minuses: Secretly in love with his stalker and doesn't really like women who talk dirty

Ask Madonna

Q: What was the best part of pregnancy?

A: The nipple-toughening exercises. A lot of women neglect them. You have to rough up those little rosebuds, get 'em ready for the onslaught. I did my nipple training ten or fifteen times a day. No baby is going to even make a dent on my boobs. I'll reveal all my secrets in my new prenatal exercise video, Nipples of Steel.

✍

Q: One thing we always hear about mothers is that they should be consistent. Since you reinvent yourself every few months and change your appearance drastically each time, will this be confusing to your child?

A: Not at all. When I was a kid, I would have killed to have my mother try even one new hairstyle. I would have loved to go to the Mizrahi show with Mom instead of Kmart. My changes in appearance will stimulate my baby. Who needs those little black-and-white mobiles when you've got Mom's outrageous eyeliner? Besides, little babies are supposed to be able to tell you by your smell—these little details like where you're living or with whom or even whether you're wearing a cone-shaped bra or baby-doll peignoir really account for very little in the large scheme of things. I doubt that an "I Dream of Jeannie" harem outfit and hairpiece will confuse a savvy infant, and I'm sure my kid will be goddamn savvy.

Q: Now that you're a mother, do you regret talking dirty to David Letterman?

A: I don't know what the fuck you're talking about.

Madonna's Maternity Quiz: Are You Ready?

A lot of people ask: M, how did you know you were ready to have a baby? Easy. I used a complex formula to decide on the perfect moment to scramble my egg. I offer this quiz here so that you can see how it is possible to evaluate your potential for parenthood. Just answer honestly (or at least in a way that your press agent deems acceptable) and then tally up your score at the end.

Lifestyle

How many lovers have you had?

1–10 (0 points)
11–25 (5 points)
26–100 (10 points)
101–235 (15 points)
236–2,000 (20 points)
2,000+ (50 points)

Score so far: ________

Give yourself 4 points for however many you own of the following:

___ bathrooms
___ cellular phones
___ NordicTracks
___ Personal trainers
___ Donna Karan tights
___ Armani suits
___ Humvees
___ Learjets
___ Versace suits
___ Jacuzzis
___ Saunas

Score so far: ________

___ How many G- or PG-rated movies have you seen in the last year? (3 points for each)

___ How many G- or PG-rated movies have you appeared in during the last three years? (7 points for each)

___ Write down the lyrics to "Can You Feel the Love Tonight?" from *The Lion King* (10 points for two lines, 20 points for more)

Rate the following activites on a scale of 1 to 10 based on how much you would enjoy them:

___ Dripping hot wax on a man's chest
___ Going to Disney World
___ Sleeping with Michael Eisner
___ Playing girls' baseball
___ Appearing on Broadway
___ Taking naked pictures of friends
___ Swearing at talk show hosts
___ Flying to Paris to buy baby clothes
___ Flying to Paris to buy a baby
___ Having an affair with the Prince of Wales
___ Doing laundry
___ Having lunch with John Gray, Tony Robbins, and John Tesh
___ Having a foursome with John Gray, Tony Robbins, and John Tesh
___ Watching Barney on TV
___ Having a threesome with Barney and Mister Rogers
___ Taking a private Learjet to the Warhol museum in Pittsburgh
___ Making a belly-button ring out of Evita Peron's hair
___ Posing for *Vanity Fair*
___ Engaging in oral sex
___ Doing a cameo on "Dr. Quinn, Medicine Woman"
___ Attending a Planet Hollywood party
___ Having an affair with Brad Pitt

___ Getting hair highlights
___ Fitting the infant car seat in the Porsche
___ Going lingerie shopping
___ Peeing in the snow in Aspen
___ Becoming the first MTV star to travel on space shuttle

Your score so far: ________

Vocabulary Section

Define the following:

1. Braxton Hicks

a. Pro-life senator from Louisiana
b. National chain of maternity-related legal services
c. Creepy little cramps that wake you up but don't mean a thing

2. Chorionic Villus Sampling (CVS)

a. Model townhouse development
b. Antibiotic-of-the-Month Club
c. Early pregnancy procedure that determines possible abnormalities, sex, and future college choice of fetus

3. Apgar Test

a. Standardized determinant of tolerance for grade-B horror movies

b. A screening process for algae in toddler wading pools
c. Test performed on baby immediately after birth to determine reflexes, respiratory readiness, and amount of obstetrician's bill

4. Onesie

a. One-size-fits-all maternity exercise leotard
b. A support group for parents of only children
c. Oversized T-shirt that snaps under baby's crotch to give her a svelte, no-panty-line look

5. Colostrum

a. Ancient stadium built for fertility rituals, recently excavated near Rome
b. New bran product designed to reduce cholesterol
c. Strange pre-milk fluid that protects your newborn from disease, allergies, and bad first marriages

6. RH Factor

a. A formula that takes the hours of postpartum REM sleep (R), multiplies it by the hours of paid help (H) you have, and predicts the number of weeks until complete mental collapse
b. An inability to master simple song lyrics, noticed in kids whose parents refuse to allow children's folksong tapes in their homes (Raffi-Holdout Factor)
c. Difficulties that occur when one parent has a positive blood type and the other a negative type or attitude

7. Breech position

a. A clause in the release forms you sign before going into the delivery room
b. Sexual technique for the last two weeks of pregnancy
c. Feet-first position of baby that indicates you will be giving birth to either a hiker or a shoe-addicted disciple of Imelda Marcos

8. VBAC

a. Adults who do not excel at children's games (Very Bad at Candyland)
b. Slang term for foxy pregnant women (Very Big and Cute)
c. Vaginal Birth After Cesarean, also known as the worst of both worlds—pelvic pain, and scarring, too!

9. Meconium

a. Latin term for any touching lullaby sung to baby between three and four in the morning
b. New antiseptic solution for boo-boos
c. An especially disgusting pre-poop substance that exudes from newborns

10. Pitocin

a. Vitamin that improves your child's chances of someday spitting out watermelon pits
b. New Gymboree-like program in which newborns swim in pits of Jell-O

c. Synthesized hormone injected into a woman's blood-stream to speed labor and sharpen contractions and her desire to murder anyone in the vicinity

Scoring: Every "C" entry is correct. One to three incorrect answers indicates a lack of maternal instincts; more than three indicates either an extreme estrogen deficiency or mental illness.

Your total score: __________

What the score means:

Nothing! The very fact that you filled out all this stuff means you want a kid bad, sister. Just hop to it, or *on* the next guy you can find.

Mommies Dearest—My Role Models

The Virgin Mary

The ultimate single mother. I was named after her, and I think she did a great job with her kid. I'll really be happy only if my kid's birthday is a national holiday and the world changes its dates back to "0" to mark the year of my baby's birth.

Medea

Okay, so she had a bad day, just like Susan Smith. But Medea stood by her convictions. Sometimes you gotta sacrifice your kids for the sake of your sexual relationship.

Lady Macbeth

A shrewd businesswoman who also looked good in a nightie.

Cleopatra

That blunt-cut hairdo was easy to care for, and she never let kids barge in between her and Caesar or Marc Antony.

Joan Crawford

A few hang-ups—wire ones, to be exact—but I'm beginning to think she was wise to opt for adoption. That way, she could concentrate on shoulder pads instead of nursing pads.

Courtney Love

An inspiration. If she can do it, so can I. Look at how little Frances Bean inspired her to do movies, too. I'm predicting that my career will get even hotter with motherhood.

Lady Madonna, or All the World's a Pregnancy Stage

I recommend taking lots of video footage during pregnancy—every stage is endlessly fascinating! I contacted my friends over at the Letterman show, and they fitted me with a Cervix-Cam so we could get those all-important close-ups during the nine preview months leading up to my baby's world debut.

1 Hour

I had the film crew come in as soon as Carlos rolled off of me: You wouldn't believe the footage I got of the sperm's Incredible Journey. It's just like a "Nova" special, only better—my egg is certainly sexier—the little sperm could barely keep his tail away from it. And isn't it just like a guy? The sperm rolled over and went to sleep, leaving my egg to do all the work for the next thirty-eight weeks. I don't even have morning sickness yet, but I'm beginning to admire lower life forms. Pregnancy in humans lasts even longer than a movie shoot. If I were an amoeba I'd be hanging out with my grandchildren already.

1 Week

I had my personal assistant go out and buy a case of pregnancy tests just so I could be extra sure. My egg is really plumping up—it's almost the size of a Lyme tick. Carlos made me do an extra hour of ab exercises—he claims that he doesn't want to see me in elastic waistbands until my fifth month.

8 Weeks

I guess I knew it would happen: Rosie and all my other friends are already getting a little bored watching the videos I'm making, and I'm starting to feel permanently bloated. Carlos can't understand why Kodak commercials make me cry. On camera, my fetus looks about the size of a cigarette butt.

12 Weeks

Carlos says that my choice of Warren Sean as a boy's name is hostile. I told him I planned to enter "Elvis Presley" in the space for father's name on the birth certificate. If I were a ferret I would have given birth by now—isn't that cool? The latest footage from the Cervix-Cam shows that the fetus is the size of plastic dog doo-doo.

20 Weeks

I passed through the awkward phase of prepartum fat and into pleasingly plump pregnancy. I haven't been this zaftig since *Desperately Seeking Susan.* Carlos is kidding that he's going to buy stock in Ben & Jerry's. (I don't recommend getting knocked up by a personal trainer—too hung up on baby fat!) Close-ups show that the fetus is the size of a Barbie doll but not as well developed. I could swear the little critter has found its good side and knows how to pose for the camera!

28 Weeks

Isn't nature wonderful? If I were an elephant I'd be only halfway to maternity. John Kennedy started rubbing my belly at a party today, but I was nearly too busy eating all the crudités to notice. The fetus has Carlos's nose and is the size of three Gouda cheese balls.

38 Weeks

Whew! No amount of personal training can prepare you for this feeling of walking around with a bowling ball between your legs. All I want to do is watch "Nick at Nite." I've only gone out dancing once this week! My belly button now has its own agent and is making late-night calls to Liz Smith. Isn't it funny? The fetus still weighs less than my left buttock but has plans to show up when most inconvenient during the next six weeks. I could swear it was thumbing its Carlos nose at me during our last taping session.

MADONNA'S FUN THINGS TO DO WITH YOUR CERVIXCAM FOOTAGE

♂ Get a copy of *2001: A Space Odyssey* and splice your baby into the giant floating fetus scene

♀ Design a Fetal Attraction video arcade game

♂ Make dupes and do a mailing to all the private preschools in your area

♀ Slip your fetal reel into the master VCR at a mega-appliance store and make everybody ogle your developing embryo

♂ Call up "Hard Copy" and tell them they can have the broadcast rights for a cool million

Who's That Girl? (or Boy?)—Finding the Perfect Baby Name

Back before I had achieved fame or fortune, I always thought I would call my kid Visa, because I believe in naming kids after someone you're indebted to. Since then, I've brainstormed many other creative ideas for naming progeny, and for years my celebrity friends have been coming to me for my self-published list of stunning, one-of-a-kind names. I'm sick to death of Dakota, Cody, Daisy, and Sophie. And I don't want to hear from anyone else who thinks I should name my kid after my record company, Maverick, or my latest blockbuster role, Evita. So I've included here a list of new strategies and sources for baby monikers. (Of course, I'm not going to reveal my very special child's name until the moment of birth.)*

---

* Note: A lot of people have been asking me if my kid will have a last name. What will it be—Ciccione or Leon? Who cares? I'm planning it so that my child will feel comfortable with just one name, as I do. It's a lot easier.

Madonna's Approved Baby Name List

Catalog Colors and Styles

I recommend scouting upscale direct-mail literature for baby names—everything from Cher's Sanctuary to Tweeds to J. Peterman. Pay close attention to the flowery descriptions of stuff you just can't live without. I particularly like the color names in catalogs. You'll notice that some of them are even those cool double names that look so good in movie credits. (By the way—don't you think that "Hammacher Schlemmer" or "Neiman-Marcus" would be really cool names, too?)

Catalog names for your baby:

Oyster
Dusty Teal
Rose Petal
Carbon Gray
Milk Chocolate
Espresso Heather
Cypress Green
Twilight Blue
Chianti Plaid
Wintergreen
Bark
Stretch Twill Jodhpurs
Industrial Blue
Lapis
Vintage Rose
Peacock

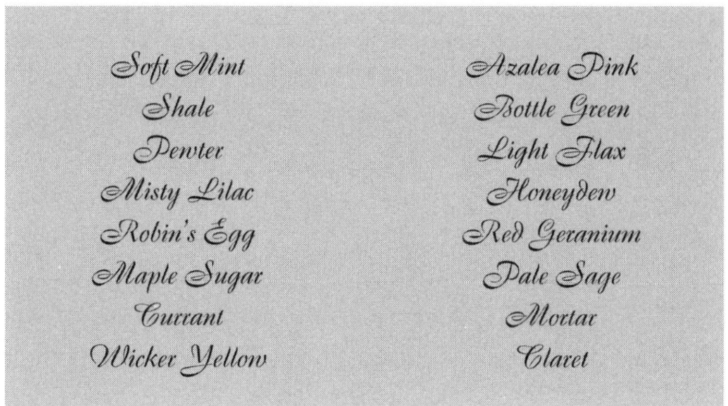

Soft Mint
Shale
Pewter
Misty Lilac
Robin's Egg
Maple Sugar
Currant
Wicker Yellow
Azalea Pink
Bottle Green
Light Flax
Honeydew
Red Geranium
Pale Sage
Mortar
Claret

Natural Category

I hardly have any time for the great outdoors, but somehow it appeals to me as a source for kids' names. First of all, natural names have a certain star charisma. (The Phoenix family had the right idea!) Basically, descriptions of wilderness items seem wholesome, natural, and hip. A few ideas:

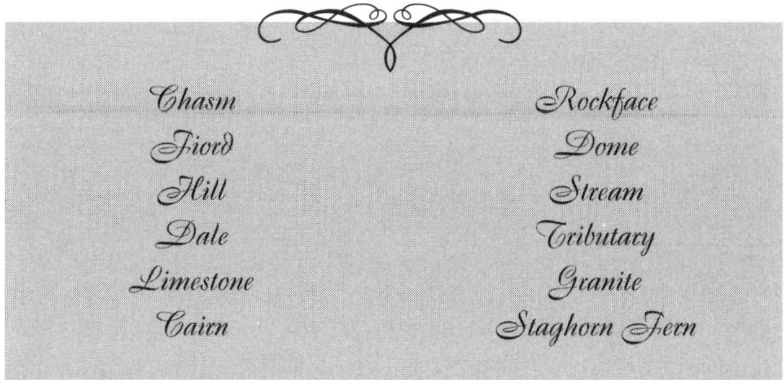

Chasm
Fiord
Hill
Dale
Limestone
Cairn
Rockface
Dome
Stream
Tributary
Granite
Staghorn Fern

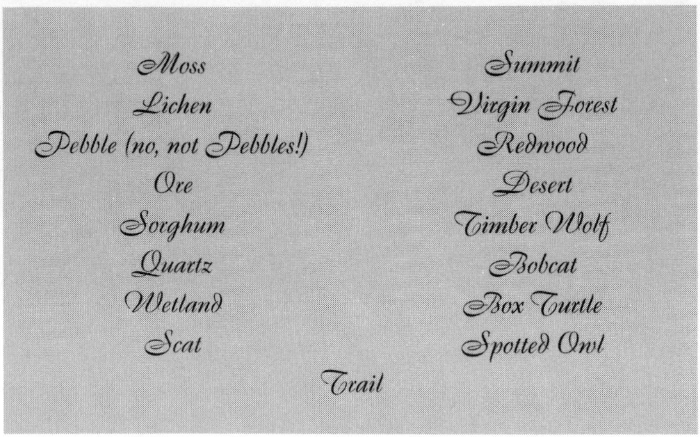

Moss
Lichen
Pebble (no, not Pebbles!)
Ore
Sorghum
Quartz
Wetland
Scat
Summit
Virgin Forest
Redwood
Desert
Timber Wolf
Bobcat
Box Turtle
Spotted Owl
Trail

Restaurants and Food Names

Let's face it: I like to dine out. I've often thought that food and sex are similarly satisfying, so why not name your kid after your favorite restaurant, chef, or dish? Some suggestions:

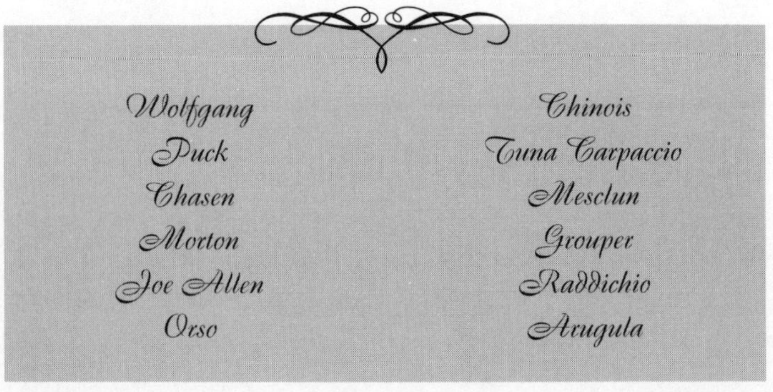

Wolfgang
Puck
Chasen
Morton
Joe Allen
Orso
Chinois
Tuna Carpaccio
Mesclun
Grouper
Raddichio
Arugula

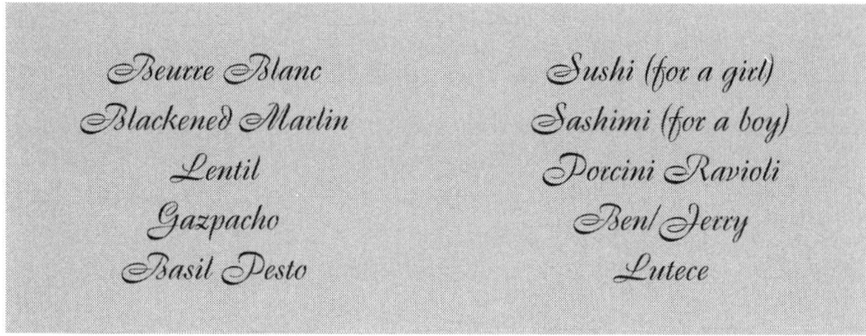

Beurre Blanc
Blackened Marlin
Lentil
Gazpacho
Basil Pesto
Sushi (for a girl)
Sashimi (for a boy)
Porcini Ravioli
Ben/Jerry
Lutece

Dance Crazes

Dance is movement. Dance is life. Dance is sex. Why not name your kid after a dance? Suggestions:

Lambada
Vogue
Macarena
Mashed Potato
Twist
Limbo
Frug

Place Names

I know a lot of stars go for the glitzy Western names like Montana and Yellowstone, but I recommend more ordinary places. I'm from New Jersey, and there are lots of naming possibilities in that state alone:

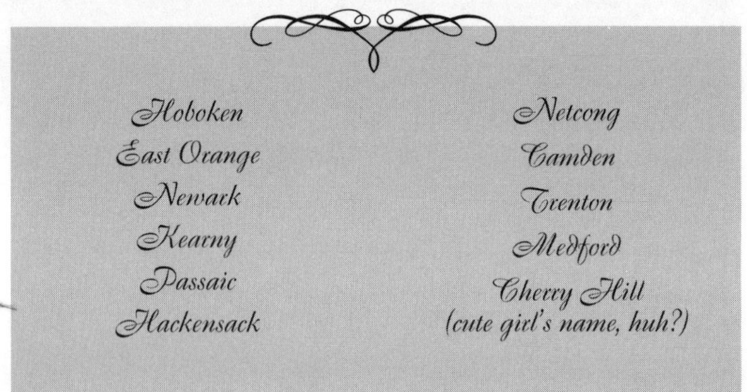

Hoboken
East Orange
Newark
Kearny
Passaic
Hackensack
Netcong
Camden
Trenton
Medford
Cherry Hill
(cute girl's name, huh?)

Madonna's Pregnancy Film Festival

As you know, I am a famous movie actress, and I like to work as a method actor. Now that I have experienced pregnancy and motherhood, I'll be able to tap into all sorts of new roles. But even if you're not planning on a celluloid parental role, you might want to check out some of these pregnant flicks. They showed me what it was really like to give birth or to interact with children. So sit back, prop up your swollen tootsies, and enjoy!

RATING SYSTEM

Four Contractions:
Better than Pitocin

Three Contractions: More Exciting Than
a Jane Fonda Postpartum Exercise Tape

Two Contractions:
Beats a Pelvic Exam

One Contraction:
As Much Fun as Peeing in a Cup

Rosemary's Baby (1968)

The grandmammy of all pregnancy angst films, starring Mia Farrow (queen of relationship angst) and John Cassavetes. The devil made her do it—he made her have his baby, and now there's hell to pay. I'm thinking of redoing my nursery to pay homage to the look of this flick, it's so cool. A completely realistic film except for that nice apartment that young struggling actor Cassavetes seems able to rent in Manhattan.

The Seventh Sign (1988)

A pregnant pre-pinup Demi Moore is haunted (no, not by Patrick Swayze) by either an emissary of the devil or an angel who wants her to know that she is carrying the Antichrist or the true Messiah. She manages to keep her makeup intact during labor and looks good even on her deathbed.

The Fly (remake, 1986)

(for fake fly birth scene only)
Dramatically portrays what it's like to give birth to a giant insect (although it could be worse, since the fly baby will surely look a little bit like Jeff Goldblum). One of the best pregnancy paranoia sequences ever filmed. But the question is never answered: Should Geena Davis get in a large supply of flypaper instead of a playpen?

The Miracle of Morgan's Creek (1944)

A drunken Betty Hutton's ovaries release too many eggs on just the right night. Madcap farcical tone cannot totally mask the horror of the final sextuplet birth sequence.

The Bad Seed (1956)

Flash forward to six-year-old murderess Patty McCormack, who is enough to scare any new mom silly:

blonde, adorable, and willing to kill a wimpy boy just for a spelling medal.

The Omen (1976)

Adoption—who knows who you'll get—a normal kid or the devil's son!! I warned my friend Rosie O'Donnell, but she still took a chance on taking in the Antichrist. It's easier to get knocked up, at least if you're thin and attractive.

Alien (1979)

(For alien-popping-out-of-stomach scene)
Every woman's nightmare of cesarean section gone awry. I can't believe that Sigourney Weaver didn't adopt after watching it over and over again on the set.

Demon Seed (1977)

The movie that asks the question: Would a computer make a better Lamaze coach than a real guy? Julie Christie mates with the computer that runs her house. Well, she'll mate with anything, even Warren. I heard there was a sequel that was never released showing her breast-feeding a laptop.

Ask Madonna

Dear Madonna,

Any tips for morning sickness? I'm having a terrible time.

First Trimester Tabitha

Dear UnoTab,

Well, I'm never up before two in the afternoon, but I assume you're talking about that vague sick feeling you get whenever you try to stand, walk, ride in a limo, or even talk on the telephone. Oh, those naughty hormones! In this case, I suggest talking to your clergy. I have a cousin who's a priest, and he gave me a two-month supply of communion wafers. Wash 'em down with San Pellegrino or Évian—they're just the thing to keep your stomach stable until you grow out of your nausea and all the garments in your closet.

Dear Madonna,

Is it okay to have liposuction during pregnancy?

Bloated in Biloxi

Dear B.B.,

Hey! The kid is riding in its own bloated sac of fluid—what can hurt it? I say, whatever makes you feel your most attractive is okay with me.

Part Two

THE SECOND TRIMESTER...

...in which I,

the very material mom,

ponder future lucrative endorsements,

consider various types of nannies,

give sex advice,

speculate on my child's former lives,

and enclose a chatty letter about

my surprise baby shower.

Kidding Myself All the Way to the Bank: The Endorsement Game

I'm not going to lie to you—I've had lousy luck getting lucrative contracts for endorsements. Nike, Adidas, and Pepsi have all courted me and then dumped me at the last minute. Why? Because I'm a wild girl, a free spirit. The corporations are worried that I'm going to embarrass them somehow.

But everyone should have at least one shot at the big advertising bucks. My situation has changed. I'm a mom. How bad can that be? I want a piece of the endorsement pie. This time, I'm not taking any chances. I hired a consulting firm, complete with scriptwriters, to scope out my possibilities. They've produced a strategic plan and spec scripts to court the most logical companies.

I've insisted on creative control. I want the spots to feature me singing and looking sexy. The maternity thing should be secondary, and none of that real wholesome crap. After all, I'm not Kathie Lee.

Take a look and see what you think.

PAMPERS
The "Papa Don't Preach" Spot

The pitch: Madonna is hip and environmentally conscious, yet she uses disposable diapers. Everyone should!

Sample Script:

```
FADE IN on buff young couple having an
earnest discussion in a beautifully
appointed black-and-white nursery. Buff
mommy is played by MADONNA; buff daddy
is played by Keanu Reeves, Johnny Depp,
or an unknown hunk. We can hear them,
but not exactly what they're saying.

CLOSE-UP of beautiful baby gurgling
and holding a round stuffed rattle
shaped like Planet Earth.

CAMERA PANS to couple, YOUNG DADDY
HUNK speaks.

          YOUNG DADDY HUNK:
   But honey, I'm worried about
   using Pampers—what about the
   environment?
```

Music swells, MADONNA gets up on changing table and begins to sing "Papa Don't Preach." She looks longingly at her husband and baby and strips down to her nursing bra.

VOICEOVER NARRATION explains how cloth diapers use up gallons of precious water and pollute our streams with detergents.

FISHER-PRICE
The "Like a Virgin" Spot

The pitch: Children are experiencing toys "for the very first time," and Madonna is the perfect woman to sell parents on the Fisher-Price line of merchandise, My First Camera, My First Pocketbook, etc.

Sample script:

OPEN ON hip Christmas scene in a Manhattan apartment with Art Deco tree and CHILDREN clustered around in Sara's Prints pajamas. HIP MOM (played by MADONNA) and HIP DAD (Antonio Banderas, Lyle Lovett, or Dermot Mulroney) smile as their progeny open up presents.

CLOSE-UP on LITTLE GIRL opening up My First Pocketbook. Music swells as HIP MOM (MADONNA) leaps up on the coffee table and begins singing "Like a Virgin . . . for the very first time" as HIP DAD looks directly into camera and talks about Fisher-Price.

HIP DAD:

Remember childhood, when you really *were* a virgin? It was cool, getting a toy for the very first time. Fisher-Price remembers, too, and you can't get a better first-time toy than our fine line of educational products. [He turns, gazes lovingly up at MADONNA] Yes—that's right, you sing it, honey!

FREEZE FRAME on ecstatic shot of MADONNA with an exquisite pout on her face, her hands on each side of her head.

VOICEOVER NARRATION:

Fisher-Price. Because we remember what it was like that very first time.

TOYS 'Я' US
The "Material Girl" Spot

The pitch: There's nothing kids like better than to be taken on a materialistic spree in a mass-market, overpriced toy store, and who better to guide them but Madonna, the original Material Girl?

Sample Script:

(Note: There will be no dialog in this commercial, just a music video look with MADONNA and A GROUP OF KIDS lip-syncing the words to her original recording of "Material Girl")

OPEN ON a typical tree-lined suburban street. KIDS are pouring out of the houses and up one particular driveway, where MADONNA waits beside a gleaming golden mini-van. She beams at the children as the sliding doors open with a whoosh and she begins singing "Material Girl." The KIDS pile in and begin singing, too. We see various scenes, including:

The van pulls up to a fast-food drive-thru; CUT TO kids happily inhaling french fries.

The van pulls into a Toys 'Я' Us parking lot; KIDS pile out, with Madonna escorting them to store's entrance.

Madonna gets oversized shopping cart, and goes Pied Piper–like throughout the aisles, getting kids whatever they want.

Madonna pulls out a $500 bill at cash register; CAMERA PANS to kids' ecstatic faces.

FREEZE FRAME on the crowd of happy children around MADONNA. Superimposed slogan reads:

TOYS 'Я' US—
WE HELP YOU LIVE IN THE MATERIAL WORLD

OTHERS WHO WILL SEEK ME OUT FOR ENDORSEMENTS AFTER PREGNANCY

Preparation H

Dodge mini-vans

The milk industry

Vlasic Pickles

Ben & Jerry's

Ask Madonna

Dear Madonna,

How can I remain sexually desirable now that I am eight months pregnant?

Tubby in Toledo

Dear Tubby,

Feeling sexy in late pregnancy is simply a matter of adjusting your fantasies. By planning ahead, you can surprise your lover with fun scenarios and costume changes:

Sexy Sumo Wrestling: He comes through the door to see that you have replaced your living room furniture with raked sand and small wooden platforms. Before he can get his bearings, you leap from behind a very large bonsai tree, your hair slicked back in a ponytail, wearing nothing but an attractive white thong. A few grunts, and you're saying "Sayonara" to the blues.

The Honeymooners: Nostalgia and sex are a potent combination when you don a bus driver's uniform and play the role of Ralph Kramden in those third-trimester lovemaking sessions. And away we go…

Fertility Goddess: You'll look ravishing swathed only in rose petals, seated in front of heaps of fatty foods, demanding obeisance. Most men adore making love to the Source of All Life on Our Planet.

My Tips: Choosing a Nanny or Caregiver

Hey, I'm only human, although a trifle superior to all of you out there. Most of my role models, like yours, come from movies and television. I've thought seriously about all of them before making my decision about child care. Here are the basic categories of video nannies from which to choose:

Fran Drescher Model

Can I be frank here? I hate this babe, with her cute squiggly body and obnoxious whine. There have been times when she's gotten almost as much press as I do. She'd never get near my kid *or* my man.

Julie Andrews Model

My absolute first choice. A musical nanny *and* a Catholic. What could be better? But she's tied up on Broadway at the moment. I've offered her gobs of money and even a special Tony, but I don't think it's going to work.

Mr. French Model

Julie Andrews in drag—only he's not as musical and he's dead.

Uncle Charlie Model

These types come in all genders—just look at Alice on "The Brady Bunch." A little too homey for my tastes. I don't really like getting that chummy with my help. I have enough older Italian relatives in New Jersey to staff a day-care center, but this is not the way to go if you want privacy.

Mammy Model

Gone with the Wind was one of my favorite movies, and Mammy was certainly a dedicated child-care worker. But my vision of the world is more Benetton than antebellum South—it just won't work for me.

Rebecca De Mornay/ Drew Barrymore Model

A definite no-no. I don't want some young thing hanging around my man.

Mrs. Doubtfire Model

This is the one I've decided on—I want someone who can take care of my kid during the day and still date me at night. Only I want him to look younger and sexier than Robin Williams.

Madonna's New Age Childbirth Techniques

Gee, isn't there anything new under the sun? I got really bored with all that Lamaze stuff and the Bradley Technique. I wanted to explore something totally different, and I have as many fantasies about childbirth as I do about sex. Here are three methods I came up with for foolproof childbirth—is anyone out there game? Maybe we can do a book!

Leary Method

As soon as you go into labor, you receive a dose of LSD that will last at least eighteen years. Would make motherhood even more of a trip than it already is.

Hotel Birthing

Couples check into that special "getaway" birthing suite. Jacuzzi, room service, bellhop obstetricians—what more could a girl want?

Fetal Bungee-Jumping

Why make birth a soothing experience, when we well know that mostly stress and risk-taking lie ahead for our offspring? Carlos and I were going to try fetal bungee-jumping until our obstetrician said his malpractice insurance wouldn't cover it. I wanted to stand on a raised platform with a big hole cut out of it and let my baby make a daring plunge into the world, bouncing by the cord and arriving to a standing ovation. It would have been a real rush!

Shanghai Surprise Baby Shower: My Very Special Day

Dear Sean and Robin,

I know you're busy with your own little brood and your very active film careers, and it probably takes hours a day just to get Sean's hair to puff up like that, but I just thought I'd write a note to let you know about how DELIRIOUSLY HAPPY I am. As you've probably heard, I'm preggers, and I managed to find myself the sperm of a calm, sane man (not that I'm casting any aspersions, Seanie—it's just that I feel *your* fetus would have ripped its way out of my womb with its bare hands) and now I'm settling in, nesting, and waiting for that big day.

Last week some of my friends, including Rosie and Inge, threw me a wonderful baby shower. They called it a "Shanghai Surprise" shower, which I thought you would get a kick out of, Sean. (Robin—in case you don't remember, that was the artistically successful film your husband and I starred in several years ago. Boy, when we used to get home from that set, let me tell you—the sex was hot! But that's another story. Hope your little kids are doing great, dear.)

Well, folks, they got me there on the pretense that we were going to watch some pornography together. I didn't suspect a thing. The "Shanghai Surprise" part of it turned out to be a really cute naked Asian guy who jumped out of the belly of a cake that looked just like me. So cool! Isn't it wonderful to have like-minded friends? I feel so fortunate. The girls had searched all over to get me unique, one-of-a-kind shower gifts. I feel as giddy and excited as I used to on Christmas morning, when I would get out my pad and pencil and write down every single gift Santa Claus brought me. So I hope you don't mind if I describe some of them for you here:

A black leather studded collar and leash for the toddler years. You know, I never really thought I'd want to walk my kid like a dog, but this collar makes it seem hip.

A case of temporary tattoo diapers. The tattoos are on the *inside* of the diapers, and when your kid pees, the tattoo affixes itself to the baby's bottom. Rosie demonstrated it on her kid Parker, and it was cute. He wet the diaper, and when she took it off, there was a perfect tattoo on his butt saying: "I Love Mom—Thanks for changing my diaper!"

Two-pound teething rings. The kid gets a workout while chomping away!

A manger cradle. My girlfriends knew how much fun it would be for me to pretend to be my namesake.

Cellular phone intercom. No dorky, clunky things for my progeny. This one comes in its own leather case and has a little Velcro strap that attaches it to baby's hand or neck. Very sophisticated.

And, of course, I got the usual other stuff—Italian baby togs, a miniature Ferrari, three Labrador retrievers, Prozac patches for postpartum depression, and assorted maternity garter belts and split-crotch panties.

It was one of the happiest days of my life, and I thought, since you two now know the pitterpat of tiny feet, that you would understand. I even thought you might send me something too, or at least a card. But I guess being an ex-wife doesn't count for anything, does it?

Now that I'm going to be a parent, too, maybe we'll see each other at some Disney opening.

Ciao, and hi to the little family!

Love,

Madonna

Reincarnation: My Top Choices for Past Babies

Do you believe in reincarnation? Sometimes I do. I think about all the wonderful things my baby might have been doing in its last life. Sure, I know some skeptics ask about where all the reincarnated dirty peasants are, but I know, *I really* know *that my baby was famous in another life, and I'll be watching that little darling closely for clues. Here are my top choices for my baby's past lives:*

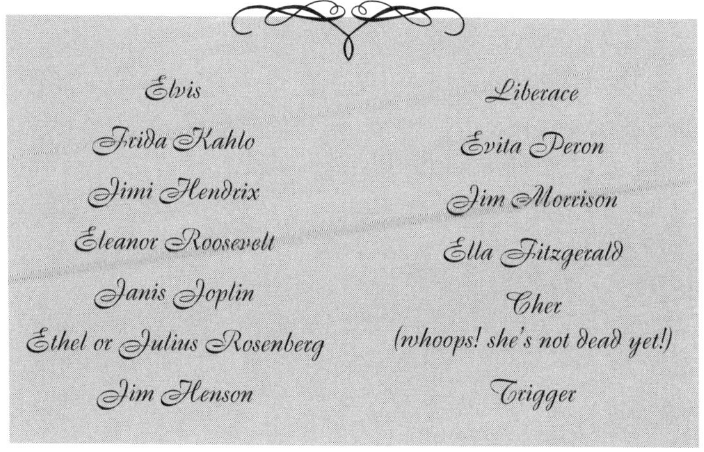

Relics of the True Madonna's Child

People have been impressed by how quiet and discreet I was during my pregnancy. I'd like to tell you it's part of my maternal instinct, but I was actually lying low planning the commercialization of my kid. I'm getting on in years, and who knows if I'll have another one? I had to figure out a strategy to make the most of everything that touches my offspring, and now I think I've got it: relics.

In case you're not a Catholic, let me explain. Relics consist of body parts, clothing, and accessories of dead sainted people and God. There are relics of the wood from the true Cross (enough, I've heard, to build a log cabin) and relics of saints' leg bones, blood, sputum, hair, and skin. My personal favorites are Saint Anthony's vocal cords, which you can see on display in Padua, Italy.

There's one basic problem with relics, of course: Most times, the person has to be dead before you can sell the relics or charge money for people to see them.

So I'm going to stretch the definition a bit when it comes to my baby. My baby's relics will be modern ones—kind of like the white disco suit John Travolta wore in Saturday Night Fever *or Archie Bunker's chair that they have on display at the Smithsonian. Babies grow fast, and I'm already collecting a bunch of stuff—my baby's castoffs—that people will want to buy. I talked to Cher, who does that cute Sanctuary catalog, for advice on how to go into direct marketing for these infant relics, and she helped me figure out prices and catalog descriptions. Here's a sample. Act now, and you can be the first to own a historic piece of my child.*

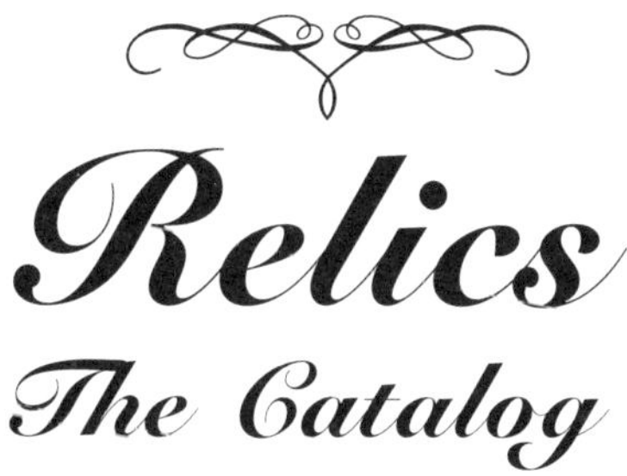

Broken Condom A rare opportunity to purchase the very condom Carlos was wearing the night I told him I wanted his baby! I had already damaged his protective shield with a needle in several places, and the rest is history. Now you can own the latex shield that launched a thousand sperm. It isn't every day that you are offered dried genetic material. It's the only THING of its kind in the world.

RUBBER2000 Broken Condom............Only $1,500

Madonna's Placenta Yes! Now you can own this **one-of-a-kind** organ, the very source of nutrients for the most famous baby on earth. Comes laminated on its own beautifully burnished brass stand with mahogany base. A certificate of ownership is included, along with an exclusive Polaroid photo of me expelling the placenta after the birth of my baby. Sure to increase in value over the years.

PLAC1996 Madonna's Placenta.................$55,000

Baby's Footprints The Limited Editions. While everyone else is content to make one of these, I got my staff to make several hundred over my baby's first few days. Be one of the few hundred people to proudly display my baby's eensy-beensy footsies on your family room wall. Ideal baby shower gift, or can be laminated and made into a high-chair food mat for your own tyke.

FEET666 Limited Edition Prints
of Baby's First Footsies..................................$575

Baby's First Fingernails Preserved forever under high-quality Plexiglas, these tiny shavings make a cute paperweight for anyone obsessed with my child or with bodily leavings. There's nothing quite as pure and innocent as baby nails—no polish, no dirt, just fresh little white reminders of days gone by. Order early—even though my nanny tried to trim my cutie pie's nails every other day, we only have a limited number of paperweights available!

NAIL2000 Nail Paperweights................$150 each

Pukey Diaper I've saved a number of 100% cotton diapers worn on my nanny's shoulder and blessed with the sacred spewings of Madonna, Jr. Since I had a wet nurse, you needn't worry about odor—even my baby's vomit smells heavenly. I've been into collecting cloth covered with body excretions ever since I took the confirmation name of Veronica, that gal who wiped the sweat off Christ's face. Hurry, because there are only 150 sacred diapers available!

PUKE911 Stained Diapers ....$200 each

Nasal Syringe Gosh—I didn't know quite what to do with this, until I got the hang of it. I darn near blew my baby's brain to smithereens, since I pumped air up the nose rather than siphoned snot out. I offer this artifact here for all similarly confused parents. Also makes a nice bellows for the barbecue, and you'll know that it touched the life of my child.

NOSEBLOW123 Nasal Syringe $125

Rectal Thermometer Oh, Lord... I feel my temperature rising! I used ten of these things during my baby's early months, and now you can own one of them for yourself. It's the thrill of knowing what a famous tush they've been in. Bottoms up!

ASS101 Rectal Thermometer $75

Madonna's Games for Children

You know, it's simply not true that I only like grown-up games like Truth or Dare. I know how to play lots of kiddie games, and I will probably be the mom most of the kids in the neighborhood like best. Here are just a few I've come up with so far, but I get new ideas every day!

Peek-A-Booby

This one is easy and a real crowd-pleaser, even for boys up to age 15. Pull up your shirt, let the child see your pointed nursing bra, and then put the shirt down. Hey—where did they go?

Pat-A-Coke

You know, I gave up coke and other drugs long ago. But I still like the paraphernalia. In this game, I snort a line of fake white powder and let baby play with the tube after I take it out of my nose. It can amuse a little rugrat for hours.

Crack the Whip

Tell baby to get down on those knees and CRAWL! as you crack a black leather whip behind him. Remember not to really hit!

Go Dish

Sit around in a circle and encourage young children to tell the most horrible stories they can imagine about each other.

Duck Duck Big Goose!

Also called Tailgate—it's a big favorite with military children.

Part Three

THE THIRD TRIMESTER...

...the home stretch,

where I'm in a league of my own

as the hippest mommy-to-be

on the block.

Here, I work out my nesting instinct,

hire a mini-entourage for baby,

look forward to my child's

developmental stages,

and give lots of valuable advice.

My Nesting Instinct Tips

Well, girlfriends, as we all know, when you get to the seventh month or so, the urge to create a new environment hits pretty hard. Suddenly you're very energetic—you just want to do something, anything. I guess it's nature's way of getting ready for the big event. Now, you could take up knitting or remodel some putrid little nursery by spray-painting teddy bear stencils on the walls, or you could do what I did: Buy real estate. Lots of it.

You see, my nesting instincts were much too large to be contained by any one real estate holding. The thrill of buying a piece of property and knowing that my baby could live anywhere on Earth perked up my last trimester considerably. I highly recommend it, especially if you employ enough flunkies to attend all the closing transactions.

So far, since I've had a bun in the oven (or, as Carlos says, "a dim sum in the wok"), I've amassed the following:

Ten Condos. Vail, Paris, Venice, London, Rio, and... uh...I forget where else.

Three Houses. Orlando (just a little pied-à-terre for Disney World), Westchester, Seattle.

Four Day-care Centers. I want to have control, in case the nanny thing doesn't work out.

Two Tour Buses and **Five Fully Equipped Mobile Homes.** Just in case I get the postpartum wanderlust.

Thirty-two State-of-the-Art Dollhouses and **Ten Miniature Railroads.** Every boy or girl—and mom—should have mini-lots of real estate with which to act out play therapy.

That's just the major stuff, of course. I've been driving my decorator brother Christopher crazy with my nursery designs for all my houses and condos around the country. We've got one Mission-style nursery, one with all the latest Milan designs, and even one S&M look at my place in Malibu. I had planned to do a nursery with a Frida Kahlo look, but Chris put his foot down, protesting, "It's almost as dated as the Keith Haring!" He doesn't know it, but I had some Frida Kahlo bumper pads made up anyway.

Ask Madonna

Dear Madonna:

My baby girl is all sort of round and "blubby." Can you recommend an exercise routine that really works?

Liposuction Lillie

Dear Lipo Lil,

You haven't told me much, but if your baby is like most others, I'm sure she has certain problem areas, like the stomach, thighs, and even neck. You're going to have to work hard with her to establish a daily routine of mat exercises, since she is probably too young to use a StairMaster or even an exercise cycle. Just send me $35.99 and a stamped, self-addressed envelope, and I will be sure that you get a new illustrated pamphlet by Carlos and me, "Babysize Your Way to Thinner Thighs in Just 30 Days." If your baby is over six months old and able to sit up, it might be time to start working her abs, too. For only three easy monthly payments of $29.95, you can be the proud owner of our new Babytummy Abdomenizer. It is designed by a NASA *space engineer, comes in Barney purple or Big Bird yellow, and virtually guarantees that your little one will have a washboard stomach within weeks.*

✍

Dear Madonna,

I got my nipples pierced last year, and now I find out I'm pregnant. Will it affect my ability to breast-feed?

Holey Mother of God

Dear Holey,

You'll be fine. Some of my friends take out their rings while in the nursing phase, but the ones who don't say that it's really convenient to have a teething ring right next to the food source.

✍

Dear Madonna,

I am worried about bonding with my baby after it is born. Any special tips?

Titters in Georgia

Dear Titters,

Don't worry so much. You'll be with your baby constantly (unless you are so wealthy, like moi, that you can afford to hire scores of wet nurses and other slaves), so bonding will probably come pretty naturally from proximity. You're going to be around it all the time—who do you expect your kid to bond with? The girl at the drive-thru window at McDonald's? The checkout guy at Seven-Eleven?

Now, as we know, I am a special case. Because of the size of my entourage, I knew I'd have to work extra hard to develop bonding rituals with my newborn. I'll let you in on a few of the things I did, and then you can adapt them to your less lustrous lifestyle.

Madonna's New Age Bonding Rituals

- ♂ In utero, always play only your own tapes for baby's listening enjoyment.
- ♀ Try to learn your baby's name in the first few weeks after birth and say it often when the baby is brought to you during photo shoots.
- ♂ Replicate the pattern of your varicose veins on your baby's legs with washable Magic Marker.
- ♀ Make a video montage of all your Letterman appearances and play it on a 54" screen in the nursery.
- ♂ Put the scab from your baby's belly button in a locket mounted in your own belly-button ring.

- ♀ Whisper the personal identification number for your home alarm system in your baby's ear as a symbol of trust.
- ♂ Have an infant seat installed on the back of your stationary bicycle so that you and baby can be together during workout time, or have weights surgically implanted into baby's feet so that you can use your tyke to pump iron.

Classified Motherhood: How I Advertised for a Mini-Entourage

Although I would never dream of doing things completely for myself, I must confess that managing an entourage can be exhausting. I need a personal entourage manager just to keep track of openings on my staff. But when it came to my baby, I knew I would want to do all the hiring myself, at least during the first year. The nanny part was the easiest (see The Second Trimester), but what about all the peripheral characters I would need to make me and my baby feel comfortable and treasured? I decided to advertise in alternative newspapers across the country—The Village Voice, The Washington City Paper, The L.A. Weekly—*to find the folks I needed to staff my infant's entourage. Here are some of my ads:*

GET IN THE SWIM!

Swimming coach needed for gifted newborn. Good benefits package and access to Olympic-size pools around the world. Salary $35,000+

ARE YOU WET? THEN WE WANT IT BAD!

Calling all lactating ladies! Several wet nurse positions available. Duties include suckling and nurturing world's most famous child. All shifts available, cute uniform included. Salary $31,000+ and all the high-carbohydrate snacks you can eat.

PERSONAL POTTY TRAINER

Grow with us—in the beginning, your position will involve some diaper duty, but then the creative part starts! Custom-designed potty chairs and the latest technology in pull-up pants will be available to you, the potty professional. Salary $40,000+ and excellent travel opportunities.

CHEERIO DISPENSER

Sensitive, caring person needed to feed Cheerios endlessly to famous tyke. Particularly interested in past experience, even if it involves animals. Salary $25,000+ and free breakfast every day.

BABY BELUGA—WE WANT YOU!

Inane singer of children's ditties sought to accompany world-famous baby on travels throughout the world. Must be familiar with all the endlessly repetitive songs, including "Itsy Bitsy Spider," "The Wheels on the Bus," "Little Bunny Foo-Foo," "Kumbaya," "Michael Row the Boat Ashore," and many others. Salary $19,000 plus career opportunities as Raffi's new sidekick.

FASHION CONSULTANT/PERSONAL SHOPPER FOR FAMOUS INFANT

Do you know the difference between Versace and Christian Dior? Do you believe babies should wear black? Would you have the personal clout to get Isaac Mizrahi or Donna Karan to design special infant garments? Come talk to us about your fashion theories for babies, and we'll see if you qualify for the dream job of a lifetime. Salary $55,000+

Madonna's Tips for Feeding the Critter

Here's a little-known truth about babies: For finishing off the contents of your refrigerator, they're even better than dogs.

After parties, my kid will live on dip leftovers. Who needs Gerber when you can feed your child sour cream onion dip? A favorite breakfast food is leftover takeout sushi plunked on the high-chair tray. Babies will even eat the "green stuff" (wasabi) until they're about a year old.

And while we're on the subject of food, don't believe this nonsense about gradually introducing foods into your kid's diet. That means that you or someone else must stand around shoveling white gruel into a little mouth for minutes on end. Nope—I like the grazing method, and I believe in the omnivore approach. That's how I was raised because of all my brothers and sisters, and I still believe it is the best training for a lifetime of cocktail parties. Once the little creature can sit up or crawl, she should be able to grab a bite to eat. Try having your staff leave plenty of edible objects in huge piles on the high-chair tray or, better yet, scattered around the floor. Watch your kid shout with glee when he or she discovers a crudité left under the Gustav Stickley table the day before.

At the Bronx Zoo the chimpanzees' keepers have started scattering food around the cage to reduce the chimps' boredom. We should adopt the same strategy for the human baby in captivity. It would alleviate the boredom of both mom and baby and put an end to all the neurotic scenes moms play out as they're trying to shovel stuff that looks like wallpaper paste down a screaming infant's throat. Let's take a banana leaf from our evolutionary junglemates: Have you ever seen a chimpanzee mom who wasted her money on a bowl with a suction cup bottom or an airplane-shaped spoon?

MY FOOD CREDOS

♀ It's never too early to learn to like sushi.

♂ Pizza crusts make excellent teething biscuits.

♀ I grew up eating white sugar, and it will do wonders for my kid, too.

♂ If something has been on the floor less than four days, it is still edible.

♀ If God had meant me to finish baby's leftovers, he would have made me a seagull.

Reality Suzuki by Madonna

Parents of preschoolers are familiar with the Suzuki method of teaching children to play the violin and cello on small-scale instruments. But is Suzuki violin a really useful skill for kids, or an especially pleasant experience for mom during practice time?

I've decided to create my own Suzuki courses for celebrity kids—certainly more appropriate!

Suzuki Agent. I've always wanted an agent who won't take "no" for an answer. With training, your young tyke could learn to negotiate the best deals for you.

Suzuki Stockbroker. Teaches the principles of investment with special editions of the *Wall Street Journal* featuring the famous "Billy Bull and Betty Bear Go to Market" stories. In just a few weeks, your tiny financial advisor will be handling your portfolio like a pro.

Suzuki Sommelier. Your child learns colors—red, white—and numbers (1982, 1986) in this fabulous hands-on program, which also introduces him to the geography of France, Australia, California, and Italy. Includes a plastic *faux* champagne bucket and a safety corkscrew.

Suzuki Housekeeper. Help your child go beyond dust-busting with this comprehensive course put together by English maids and butlers. A new kind of potty training that will leave your bathroom in tip-top shape.

Suzuki Personal Trainer. Young children are always around the house, so why not let them put you through your paces? Then you can fire their good-for-nothing fathers and combine personal fitness with mother–child quality time together.

Ask Madonna

Dear Madonna,

I have been experiencing a lot of difficulty separating from my three-year-old. Any tips?

Anxious in Alabama

Dear Anxious,

A lot of my more maternal friends complain of separation anxiety. Perhaps the best cure is to think about all the ways in which you really are a separate person and not at all like a sniveling preschooler.

Here's my imagined list, and I encourage you to make up your own.

DIFFERENCES BETWEEN ME AND A THREE-YEAR-OLD

1. I can think of only one activity that, when it's over, I feel like saying, "Let's do it again!"
2. I get bored after my fourth viewing of "Big Bird Goes to China."
3. I like my pizza hot.
4. I can color inside the lines.
5. I like pornography.

Dear Madonna,

I get embarrassed when people see that my four-year-old is still sucking on a pacifier. Little old ladies come up to me in shopping malls and scold me for being a bad mother. What can I do?

Binkies Anonymous

Dear Binkies,

Yes, little children do persist with disgusting habits that make us look bad, don't they? That's why I've perfected my new over-the-counter line of Madonna's ToddlerDerm skin patches. They treat these addictions invisibly, alleviating parental discomfort. The patches come decorated with cartoon characters—kids love 'em. Here's one that will solve your problem quickly, plus a few others for common yet embarrassingly childish behavior.

<u>SuckerDerm</u>—Placed on arm, patch completely eliminates child's addiction to thumb or pacifier sucking.

<u>BlankieDerm</u>—Made from an actual tiny patch of your child's security blanket affixed to a porous backing. Attaches to the tummy to dispense that safe feeling a kid craves. Now no one needs to see pathetically filthy fabric remnants dragged along the ground. And your tyke won't ever lose BlankieDerm!

<u>DroolawayDerm</u>—Special pink-colored patch is placed inside the throat to eliminate that Wet Look.

Fighting the Prego Blues: Some Tips

Not everything about being pregnant is fun or even upbeat. Occasionally those hormones get the better of you, and you want to kill those around you or even the thing inside you. When that happened to me, I just put on my New Age "Peaceful Evening" CD, breathed deeply, and meditated. I tried to soften my hostility toward the World's Most Famous Fetus and toward pregnancy itself by finding constructive activities.

Things to Do When You're Feeling Blue and Pregnant

♂ Call 911 and report the fetus as a stalker.

♀ Get a copy of the *New York Times Magazine* and write away for applications to all the boarding schools listed in the back.

♂ Send your lover to Thailand for the perfect spring rolls.

♀ Read Lorena Bobbitt's biography.

♂ Call *Vanity Fair* and demand a nude prego photo shoot—you're cuter than Demi Moore!

♀ Call your high school sex education teacher in the middle of the night and make death threats.

Madonna's Milestones of Early Celebrity Childhood

Don't let anyone fool you—celebrity children really are different, and no baby book is going to give you the real information you need on how to gauge your kid's development. From talking to friends, I have been able to outline a few of the essential stages you'll notice in the typical famous child. My baby, of course, is reaching every single one of them months before schedule.

Responds to Mom's Videos (16 to 18 months). The onset of television addiction is a great sign that your tyke is going to follow in your famous footsteps. Make sure that the first tapes your kid sees are of yourself, dancing and looking perky. The true signs of a celebrity kid's involvement with future fame—open mouth; direct, vacant stare at the screen—can be a very moving moment. (Plus, you'll want to pave the way for those all-important guest appearances on "Sesame Street.")

Discovers Cameras (from 12 months on). Opens up a world of photo ops. From this time on, be sure to plan outfits accordingly.

Responds to Bribery (from 19 months on). Nature knows what it's doing. Bribery responsiveness develops at about the same time the child might get its first movie role offer. With just a few Tootsie Rolls, you can talk your kid into a lucrative contract.

Pays First False Compliment (from 25 months on). Typical first line, "You're so beautiful, Mom." This Eddie Haskell behavior pattern is an important step in mental development. Your child, growing progressively less cute as it ages, realizes that verbal skills will now play an important role in self-preservation. You should record as many comments like these as possible, and play them over for yourself thirty years later when the kid has published the tell-all memoir.

Becomes Obsessed with Genitals (15 months to end of life). Hey, I've made a career out of this skill, and I intend to foster it in my offspring. Posing nude can bring a lot of money.

Tells First Obnoxiously Repetitious Anecdote (17 months and up). Let's suppose it's some droll, amusing story about how your kid's shoe fell into the river otter's cage at the zoo and the animal swam laps with it. Remember, this could be your chance to write a children's book. Fergie did it. Ally Sheedy did it. The children's book market is the place to be. So listen to those boring little stories, hire an illustrator, and get cracking!

Learns to Whine (36 months and on and on and on). It takes the human vocal cords a few years to be able to produce a sound so like fingernails on Styrofoam. There is the cheap whine, which can be remedied by small trinkets at the checkout counter, or the more mature, vintage whine, which addresses all the wrongs you've ever perpetrated upon the child. A celebrity child should be a good whiner—it makes for fabulous copy later in life.

Begins to Leverage Guilt (32 months 'til forever). You will recognize the onset of this phase by key phrases: "Don't leave me, Mommy!" "You said you were coming home early—were you out with your new boyfriend?" Worst of all, your kid will attempt to undermine your sense of self-worth by citing lesser celebrities' motherhood skills: "Deborah Harry's kid gets picked up at one o'clock!"

Has a Soft Drink or Fried Chicken Nugget Dinner Named After Her at a Hollywood Theme Restaurant (22 months on). True sign of celebrity child arrival.

Recognizes Car Models (31 months). Your kid should begin recognizing the difference between a Lexus and a Toyota at a very early age. Take her through restaurant and mall parking lots and emphasize Jaguars, Porsches, Humvees, and Rolls-Royces—she'll get the idea.

Dials First Long-Distance Number (26 months). Once baby dials the coast, you know it's time for "My First Cellular Phone."

Gets First Agent (birth to 5 years). Every child should have one, if only to negotiate with Mom and Dad.

SPECIAL CELEB-KID IMMUNIZATIONS I'D LIKE TO SEE

I know that shots are an important part of the pediatric regimen for the first year of baby's life. But is the current repertoire of immunizations, designed to guard against all those old musty diseases, really enough preparation for the celebrity child? I won't feel safe until my precious one gets these:

Drew Barrymore/Dweezil Zappa Syndrome (DBDZS) Shot. Given at three months of age. Prevents your child from failing to make a living as a performance artist, painter, poet, actor, or musician. A special booster shot one year later, MBA (Make Bucks Always), ensures a six-figure income in spite of offspring's low talent level.

Weasels Shot. Given at fourth year checkup. Protects your offspring from falling in with the wrong crowd in school and, later, at all the cool dance clubs.

Delirium, Passion, Titillation (DPT) Shot. Administered at eight months, vaccinates child against future disappointing love affairs and boring opening night party conversations.

Folio Serum. Enables child to read original Shakespearean documents at age of two and get Hollywood backing for his or her own production of *Henry V* soon after kindergarten. (Kenneth Branagh's parents had him inoculated with this, and it worked just fine.)

Baby P.R.: How to Understand and Unlock Your Kid's Potential

All actors have known for years to avoid playing scenes with babies and dogs. That's because both tykes and pets are naturals at public relations strategies. All a parent needs to do is tap into this P.R. power, and you'll see all sorts of opportunities materializing for your kid. Here are some I've noticed already:

Eye Contact: Wow! My baby fixes its little eyes on me like crazy. All babies use this technique, like any good salesman or fan. Fortunately, new babies cannot yet repeat your name over and over while they are staring at you.

Smiling: Most adults fall for this every time. A baby develops a range of mouth movements that can convince those special adults in his life that he has a unique smile in his repertoire just for them.

Googling: In this brilliant verbal strategy, babies take a page from cats, who understand the absolute power of making a constant, soothing sound for owners' ears.

Addiction: Nothing flatters like someone who bursts into tears the moment you leave the room and who chants your name over and over. We're talkin' great P.R.!

Motherhood: The Future

Well, friends, it has been fun sharing my thoughts, prejudices, and opinions with you. As I look forward to the wonderful months and years of maternal bliss ahead of me, I can see so many opportunities for me and my child:

- ♂ Sitcoms: Either single-mom stuff with my adorable tyke; or a Freddie Prinz–type show with Carlos running a gym and coming home to his Lucy-like spouse, me.
- ♀ Celebrity memoirs by my kid and me, detailing our great love for each other (or, if we agree, a real hate-match that will get us lots of ink!).
- ♂ Cracker and cereal commercials and endless infomercials for the two of us, extolling the benefits of storage units, building blocks, and phonics reading programs.

♀ Kids' albums, featuring smarmy remakes of favorite songs from the seventies. (Sample: "If you want my diaper, and you think it's poopy... c'mon Mommy let me know!")

And that's just the beginning.

So, thanks, reader—and may all your gestational experiences be the best!

Love,

Madonna